Lead, Follow, or Get Out of the Way

An Avant® Leadership Guide

Lead, Follow, or Get Out of the Way

Leadership Strategies for the thoroughly Modern Manager

James L. Lundy

Avant Books®
San Marcos, California

Library of Congress Cataloging-in-Publication Data

Lundy, James L.
Lead, follow, or get out of the way.

1. Leadership 2. Management. I. Title
HD57.7.L86   1986   658.4'092   86-10065
ISBN 0-932238-49-1

Avant Books®
Slawson Communications, Inc.
165 Vallecitos de Oro
San Marcos, CA 92069-1436

Interior Design by Sandra Mewshaw
Cover Design by Lorri Maida
Art by Estay Heustis

10 9 8 7 6 5 4 3 2 1

This book is dedicated to all who are interested in improving performance and results through better communication and understanding.

Contents

Memorandum I

Major Challenges Exist
for
Those Who Would Be Leaders

Item 1

Some Questions—and a Preview

Do you believe that more people should listen to you?

Among those who *do* listen to you, should most listen better?

Do you sometimes feel that others push too hard to convince you of their points of view instead of seeking mutual understanding?

Have you ever thought you could have been more inspired to do something if you had been asked instead of ordered?

Could the departments in your organization do a better job of communicating, cooperating, and collaborating?

Would your life be more pleasant, and would you be more productive if you had fewer misunderstandings with your supervisors, peers, subordinates, customers, vendors, and others?

If you have answered yes to most of these questions, you understand the need for this book. As you read it, you may want to think about whom you know who might benefit most from it.

Let's consider a few additional—and very important—questions.

Who are all these people who don't listen to you as much as they should and who could be more cooperative? Are they the same ones who don't listen to and cooperate with me? Is it possible that we—you and I—are sometimes they?

And is it likely that we would all be better off if each of us asked more questions and listened better? Tolstoy demonstrated keen insight when he admonished that:

> *Everyone wants to change humanity,*
> *but nobody wants to change himself.*

The two sets of questions you have just read may well be the most significant materials in this book. You might consider re-reading them slowly while reflecting carefully about their purpose and potential value.

The rest of this book explores those aspects of leadership in which you probably wish your supervisor were more effective. Could they be the same aspects of leadership in which your subordinates wish *you* were more effective?

Item 2

The Subordinates' Lament

Throughout many—or maybe even most—organizations you can frequently hear the subordinates' lament. Although the exact phraseology may vary, the general message remains:

We the uninformed,
working for the inaccessible,
are doing the impossible
for the ungrateful!

Well-meaning, dedicated, and hard-working though a manager may be, his or her subordinates need to feel involved, understood, and appreciated. The better they are as subordinates, the more they expect to know about what is going on; and the more they deserve to know, the more frustrated they are when they don't know.

A stress expert claims that most of the people in our country don't like their work. (And most don't like their spouses, which means, apparently, that most of us neither want to go to work nor want to go home!) What causes so many people to be less than fully enthusiastic about their jobs?

Certainly there are many variables, but one key consideration must be the style and adequacy of leaders. Whether we are operators evaluating our first-level supervisors (throughout this book the words supervisor and manager are used to describe anyone—including the company officers—who has subordinates) or vice presidents discussing our president, most of us feel that we should know the answer to:

Where is the company headed?
What is my role in this effort?
How is my performance going to be evaluated?
How am I doing?

And we want more than just being told, told, told! We want to be asked to think—we want to be involved in the decision-making process.

We want access to our supervisors, input into the setting of objectives, and recognition for achievements.

Don't you want your supervisor to be communicative, available, supportive, open to suggestions, willing to delegate, and appreciative of your efforts?

Now switch roles. How do you interact with your subordinates? Ask yourself these key questions:

> *How am I doing as a leader?*
> *Would my subordinates identify with the*
> *subordinates' lament?*
> *How could I be more effective as a leader?*
> *How would I like to work for me?*

How about it? How would you like to have yourself as a supervisor?

Item 3

Choosing Between Authoritarian Management and Participative Leadership

It's a matter of style.

Authoritarian managers are task-oriented and prone to rely on their position of authority when directing their subordinates. They leave little or no room for their subordinates to contribute to the decision-making process. In the extreme, these managers expect subordinates to follow orders without ever challenging them or questioning the command.

By contrast, participative leaders create an open atmosphere. They solicit input from subordinates at the very beginning of the decision-making process. But don't misunderstand; they are not asking subordinates to vote on matters affecting them or their departments. Instead, participative leaders want the benefit of subordinates' thoughts before making a decision.

Whether or not you choose to pursue a more participative style is up to you. Certainly organizations have cultures, and the particular environment you work in is one variable affecting your style. In fact, a dictatorial environment emanating from the top of an organization may almost preclude using a highly participative style lower in the hierarchy. Nevertheless, room normally exists for individuals to shift toward participative leadership—at least to some degree.

Unfortunately, when we have problems communicating or interacting, we tend to blame the environment or someone else—but not ourselves. How easy it is to settle for an attitude such as: *I wish the departments in our company would be more communicative and cooperative with us.* Or: *I wish others would listen to me.* Instead, each of us should be asking how well we listen to, communicate with, understand, cooperate and collaborate with, praise, and appreciate others.

Not long ago an engineering manager heard that he was viewed as uncooperative, someone less than a team player. But he was loyal to the company and dedicated to his job—he typically worked twelve to fourteen hours a day. He apparently didn't want to be uncooperative, and he was concerned that he was viewed as being that way.

As we discussed his concern, he kept focusing on *them* and *they*. It was quite some time before he was able to focus on himself, and on *his* behavior, as a contributing factor. We explored questions like these: Do you ever set aside your own priorities and simply stroll into another department for a few minutes to greet those in the other department, ask how they are doing, and ask if you can be of any help? Could you pay more attention to the needs and interests of others? Do you usually consider fairly the requests of others that might inconvenience you or your department, or do you tend to give a quick negative response? Eventually, he began to realize why others perceived him the way they did.

You, too, can choose to cultivate more teamwork and improve your leadership style. Perhaps you feel that your subordinates misunderstand you too frequently or that they lack your high level of commitment and dedication. You may also sense lower morale among them than you would like—perhaps even hostility. If these issues concern you, consider shifting toward a more participative style.

It's a matter of style!

Item 4

What Characteristics Do Subordinates Desire and Respect in Leaders?

In what respects do you consider yourself to be a good leader? What characteristics do you have that contribute to your ability to lead? How about others who have supervised you, or whose leadership you have had an opportunity to observe? Which of their leadership traits have you admired?

Take a moment to list six to ten of the traits you desire and respect in leaders.

Characteristics That Contribute to My Respect for Leaders:

1._____
2._____
3._____
4._____
5._____
6._____
7._____
8._____
9._____
10._____

On the next page are the leadership traits most frequently identified by over two thousand managers in surveys that our firm conducted between 1980 and 1984. Survey participants were asked to list six to ten characteristics that contribute to their respect of leaders. (We did not ask that the traits be ranked in order of importance.)

Characteristics of Leaders	% of Responses
1. Communicates, allows input, is willing to listen.	11
2. Is interested, appreciative, complimentary, supportive, humanistic, considerate.	10
3. Displays honesty, integrity, trustworthiness.	10
4. Is objective, open-minded, tolerant, rational, reasonable, fair.	9
5. Delegates, trusts subordinates, allows room to achieve.	8
6. Motivates, challenges, inspires, is team-oriented.	7
7. Is knowledgeable, experienced, competent, intelligent, has good judgement.	6
8. Is available, approachable; provides feedback; trains, coaches.	5
9. Is constructive, enthusiastic, positive, friendly, humorous.	5
10. Is decisive, courageous; takes risks; is willing to commit.	5
11. Is goal-oriented, makes plans, clarifies expectations, follows through.	4
12. Accepts responsibility, blame; admits errors; is respected, respectful.	3
13. Is a doer, participates, sets example.	3
14. Is open, candid, sincere, credible.	3
15. Is tactful, humble, sensitive, understanding.	3
16. Sets high standards; is dedicated, hard-working, reliable.	3
17. Is consistent, even-tempered.	3
18. Is organized, structured.	2
19. Is creative, resourceful; has vision.	1
20. Other.	1

Notice that the item at the top of the list is a basic element in participative leadership. In fact, all but a few of the traits in the list relate to participative leadership.

How does your list compare to this one? Do you, as a supervisor, embody most of these traits? Or do some of them warrant more of your attention?

Item 5

Teamwork Through Individual Commitment

It's a rare organization in which teamwork is perceived as adequate and an even rarer one in which teamwork could not be improved. With concerted effort, people within an organization can substantially improve the extent to which various groups communicate, cooperate, and collaborate.

Retaining a high level of teamwork, however, requires constant attention and effort by each individual involved. This constitutes a universal and fundamental management challenge.

In leadership workshops, people have consistently and dramatically demonstrated their tendency to develop loyalties to subgroups rather than to the organization—or group—as a whole. In a workshop conducted several years ago for forty managers, the participants were divided into five groups of eight members each with members from each department spread among the groups. Each group was allowed twenty minutes to develop five recommendations for improving interdepartmental teamwork. Then each group was given a felt pen in a different color so it could outline, in its own distinct color, five suggestions for improvement.

At the end of the twenty minutes, the recommendations of all five groups were taped to the wall. Four of the groups made five suggestions, but one, the green group, provided only three.

Following the reports, the various suggestions (most of which were quite good) were discussed. Then the groups voted, by a show of hands, on which had the best set of recommendations. Each group received exactly eight votes; everyone in the room, without exception, voted for his or her own group. Even the members of the green group voted for themselves, in spite of the fact that they had completed only sixty percent of the assignment!

Nobody opted to look at the big picture by saying: "Gee—it looks to me as if all the reports are good! Do we really have to select one of them as best?" And, of course, nobody risked being seen as a traitor by voting for a group other than his or her own.

In setting up these groups, which in essence constituted five new departments, subgroup loyalties developed to a sufficient degree that a we-they attitude was present in everyone in just twenty minutes. It is no surprise, therefore, that such attitudes are exhibited among people who work together for many years in organizational subgroups—sections, departments, or divisions.

It's not that subgroup loyalties are bad in and of themselves. Loyalties develop because people enjoy a feeling of belonging. Most of us appreciate—and even need—the comfort of feeling we are part of a group. It is comforting to know that our associates not only accept us but also care about us and can, in all probability, be counted on to help in times of need.

We must recognize, therefore, that subgroup loyalties evolve; they are a fact of life. The leader's challenge is to recognize this fact, accept it, and try to keep each individual aware of the overall needs of the enterprise. In other words, the leader's job is to make sure that subgroup involvements don't get in the way of the organization's overall success.

The effective leader constantly works to cultivate the individual's commitment to the organization by demonstrating that the real team to which an individual belongs is more than just his or her section, department, or division.

On Teamwork

The purpose of an organization is to achieve overall effectiveness, not just the effective performance of individual groups. We must all strive to do well individually, yet always with a focus on the overall needs of the organization.

Everybody, according to Tolstoy, wants to change humanity—but nobody wants to change himself or herself. We must look for ways to compliment and support others, not blame one another for our difficulties.

Anyone can dedicate himself or herself to long hours, hard work, and individual effectiveness—and feel good about his or her contribution. The true issue, however, is the extent to which we contribute to the goals and results of the organization as a whole.

Management must recognize people's tendency to identify with groups and the extent to which they quickly develop small group loyalties. One of management's key challenges, therefore, is to help broaden the scope of vision beyond the interests of the individual unit, department, or division.

We will never be better as a company than we are to each other. As we look beyond our conveniently narrow horizons, we should continually ask how we can be of help, and we should never implement a change without previously reviewing it with others who might be affected by the change.

Opportunities to help one another, person-to-person and department-to-department, are all around us. They are amazingly easy to find if we keep watching for them, and if we make it a habit to ask people in other departments how they are doing—and how we can be of help.

Real teamwork can be so gratifying that it may be considered reward enough. Nevertheless, the individual who habitually communicates, cooperates, and collaborates with others will be recognized by his or her associates as an individual asset.

Knowledge of where the organization is headed, what each individual's general role is in the overall endeavor, and what specific objectives particular groups are expected to achieve is extremely important. For optimal success of the organization, however, a spirit of teamwork is absolutely essential!

Item 6

Investing in Process

In a seminar several years ago, a division manager from a major corporation was wrestling with feedback about the way he communicated with his associates. The other participants were coaching him on ways he might become more effective.

After a few minutes, the manager began to smile. He even seemed to sparkle a little as he said, "What you're helping me to understand is that *how* I say something may be as important as what I say!"

You bet! At that point the room seemed to glow—and the manager's life was destined to change! In fact, before the seminar, the manager's supervisor had told me that unless that particular participant improved his interpersonal relations, it was unlikely that he would be promoted again. This story ends, however, on a happy note; six months later the manager was promoted to director.

The participant's conclusion that the way something is said may be as important as what is said reflected his new insight into the difference between content (what is said) and process (how it is said). In fact, his conclusion is probably an understatement: How something is said may actually be *more* important than what is said!

When the way that something is said (process) conveys a different meaning than the actual words (content), the interpretation triggered by the process will prevail. For example, when two old friends meet after many years of separation, one might say "George, you old s.o.b.!" The words themselves are negative, but if they are spoken with a ring in the voice, George will have no doubt that his friend is delighted to see him.

With sarcastic comments, too, the way things are said overrides the meanings of the words themselves. Negative intonation has the power to dominate positive words.

You might want to flip back to the list of leadership traits and note how many of the positive characteristics of leaders pertain to process—or the way a supervisor uses his or her knowledge. In fact, only the seventh item (is knowledgeable, experienced, competent, intelligent; has good judgement) is clearly content oriented—and it only accounted for six percent of the response. All the other responses pertain to the way a leader interacts with others.

But what about those who argue that content is all-important? "I may not have time to worry about how I say something," the content-oriented manager points out. "It's much faster to be brief and concise and get on with the work at hand. What's right is right, and that's all that should matter!"

When trying to build and strengthen interpersonal relationships, an attitude that "What's right is right" can be absolutely wrong. We may be able to make no better investment than the small amount of time and effort required to improve the way things are said and done.

Certainly, some conditions require quick authoritarian action. In the event of a fire, for example, even a highly participative leader would be likely to holler "Fire!" and direct people's actions according to the needs of the situation.

And when bullets are flying, military officers can be expected to bark orders. However, during noncritical periods, such as when they and their men are simply marking time, the best leaders often interact in a participative way. Those who don't—the ones who are seen as dictatorial and arbitrary—traditionally have been labeled as such by their men. They are the kind of officer whose lives may be at risk during chaotic crises. Rumors have existed in all wars about less than great leaders whose lives may have been taken opportunistically by their own troops.

One chief executive whose major skill was the way he interacted with others achieved an incredible increase in corporate performance by simply changing the authoritative corporate culture to one best characterized as well-coordinated teamwork. For thirty years the organization had been run by the creative founder (a real genius) who made all the decisions himself and then dictated operating instructions to his three submissive (but frustrated) lieutenants.

When the new chief executive took over he began welding a team by allowing input from the key subordinates before making any major policy or strategy decisions. He looked forward to challenges and opportunities rather than backward to blame. When one department manager criticized or cast aspersions on another, the chief executive immediately called in the other person so the issue could be openly discused and resolved. The key subordinates soon learned that it was better to resolve their differences constructively among themselves than to try to throw darts at each other. With this new approach, a company that had grown between 10 and 20 percent a year for 30 years exploded during the next 4 years with volume and profit increases of more then 400 percent.

It's awfully easy in the short run to make quick decisions on our own, to be curt and directive in giving instructions, to be demeaning or even insulting when being critical of others, and to be argumentative while winning arguments—and damaging relationships. However, it takes incredibly little additional time and effort to allow others to contribute their thoughts on pending decisions, to encourage involvement, to ask for commitments instead of demanding them, to be constructive and supportive when seeking improvement, and to be able to disagree without being disagreeable—and thus to capitalize on the creative ideas and support of all those who can contribute to making good things happen.

What it *does* take to improve the way one interacts is the appropriate attitude toward others. An understanding of their desires and needs, when coupled with nominal investments of time and effort in the short run, will yield wonderful long-term returns. The increases in morale and teamwork will lead to improved performance and results.

A person who is bright, knowledgeable, dedicated, decisive, and dependable may also be understandably impatient and intolerant when dealing with others of average ability. But it is just such a person who may get the nod for promotion into first-level supervision—where the focus on results must be expanded to encompass relationships. We'll explore the factors critical to successful leadership, the methods successful leaders use to achieve optimum performance from their key people, and the potential rewards that can be expected from investments in process.

"What's right is right," can be absolutely wrong!

Memorandum II

It's Easy to Get Off to a Poor Start

1. The Making of a Supervisor or Manager

2. The Myth of the Eight D's of Supervision

3. The Ultimate Definition of a Leader

Item 1

The Making of a Supervisor
or Manager

In response to the question: "How do you create a supervisor?" a key executive in a high-tech organization once replied. "It's easy—you just change the color of his or her badge." He was being facetious, of course. Becoming a supervisor is not so easy.

You've already heard the subordinates' lament. But supervisors have been known to register a complaint as well:

> *Supervisors are often blamed,*
> *But are seldom (or inadequately) trained.*

In most organizations, first-level supervisors tend to be promoted with little or no leadership training. If you survey their subordinates, the response is usually that whatever leadership training there was, it wasn't enough!

Functional specialists—such as engineers, accountants, or sales people—may spend years learning their field of expertise. Yet when they get their first supervisory promotions, they often are plunged into the complex world of supervisor-subordinate relations and interdepartmental cooperation without the necessary preparation. Many soon get an abrupt orientation to the old adage: "Management would be easy if it weren't for people!"

Whereas mathematical formulas and the laws of physical and chemical science provide the basis for predicting the behavior of things, people are infinitely variable and thus less predictable. A leader's mission is to understand individual differences and to be able to marshal people's collective resources for effective performance. And that's not an easy task. It requires specialized skills beyond those learned by functional experts.

Recall—or imagine—what it was like to select someone for promotion into the ranks of supervision. Whom did you pick? What were the characteristics of the leading candidates for consideration? Were most of them high producers in their own specialities—for instance, the leading salespeople? Did you consider promoting anyone who produced less but who may have had other attributes, such as listening skills and a strong orientation to teamwork? Or did you feel that the promotion should be a reward given to the highest producer?

Your answer to these questions may reveal that your decision to promote a certain candidate over another is based on incomplete—if not inappropriate—criteria. The highest producer doesn't necessarily embody the strongest supervisory skills—at least not without the proper training.

Item 2

The Myth of the Eight D's
of Supervision

When reviewing people in order to select one for promotion, most supervisors take a reasonably simple approach but do not always meet with success. That approach is based on the assumption that *you* are pretty good as a supervisor. And because you supervise about as well as anyone else you know, why not look for someone pretty much like you? This is called hiring or promoting in your own image.

How do you know you're so good? You match the eight d's of supervision.

- Dedicated
- Dependable
- Demanding
- Doer
- Decisive
- Determined
- Deep Thinker
- Darn good

Sure enough, you can be pretty proud of yourself! And, fortunately, one of your people measures up to these eight factors just about as well as you do. What a break!

But since the creation of a new supervisor is such an important matter, you proceed cautiously, considering each factor carefully:

Dedicated? You bet. She diligently, almost blindly, supports your decisions.

Dependable? Absolutely. She does exactly what you tell her, and she almost never lets you down.

Demanding? Yes. She has repeatedly pushed her associates to try to match her own high expectations for herself but has been able to control her impatience and intolerance reasonably well.

Doer? And then some! She doesn't waste time hanging around the lunch room or engaging in any chit-chat. She's a real producer.

Decisive? She certainly has been so far. She knows the operations and how they should run, and she can be counted on for quick answers when asked.

Determined? Why not? She knows what she's doing and sticks to her guns. If asked to explain why, she's confident enough to reply, "Because that's the way it should be done."

Deep thinker? Apparently. She works well by herself and doesn't bother others with a lot of questions.

Darn good? She must be! She gets the job done—and doesn't take any sass from anyone.

So you've made a preliminary decision. You've reviewed it in your own mind, and you're comfortable with it. Then you approach the lucky person and say, "I've watched you perform, and I've been pleased, so I'm going to promote you to supervisor starting right now!"

Bang! A few minutes ago she was just an employee. And suddenly she's *somebody*. She's now the boss! Maybe just a junior boss, but a boss nevertheless.

And don't think she doesn't understand fully how she achieved this new-found success. You were pleased with the way she fulfilled the eight d's, so the eight d's it will continue to be. Perhaps even in spades!

And so it comes to pass. A new supervisor has been created. Oh, yes. One more thing:

Don't forget to change the color of her badge!

3

The Ultimate Definition
of a Leader

Each time you create a new supervisor, you expand the ranks of your management team. But do you have one more leader? In fact, do you have *any* leaders in your supervisory/managerial ranks?

Your team includes a chairman, a president, a few vice presidents, even more managers, and quite a number of supervisors. But which ones—if any—are leaders?

Leadership is not a function of titles; it is a function of relationships.

What about the outlook for the young woman whose promotion we just witnessed? Should we give her some leadership training to prepare her better for handling her new responsibilities?

Perhaps there's no time for that right now. There's a job to be done, and we've found our supervisor—so let's get on with it! We'll give her some leadership training when we get a chance.

She probably realizes that her own conformation to the eight d's got her into supervision, so she is likely to continue in her quiet, non-communicative ways while expecting high levels of performance from herself—and now from her subordinates, as well. Thus she is likely to be viewed as a driver, not as a leader.

Leadership has been defined numerous times, but only one definition stands the test of careful scrutiny. Whether or not this woman ever becomes a leader depends solely on whether she can fulfill the ultimate criterion of a leader.

A leader is anyone who has followers. Conversely, regardless of title, you *cannot* be a leader *without* followers!

A person who has subordinates but not followers is not a leader. Subordinates who are not followers may be viewed as resources to be managed—and that's just the view taken by a supervisor who is not a leader.

Have you ever worked for a supervisor who was not a good leader: Someone who didn't seek your input, wouldn't listen, barked orders, and was too busy to give compliments or say thanks? The chances are that you have worked under such a person at some time. Did you feel good about your job in general? Were you inspired to do your very best? Did you have feelings of achievement?

Would you like to continue in such an atmosphere, or go back to it, whichever the case may be? Would you recommend it to others? Probably not.

Once again, you might want to examine your own style and ask yourself some additional questions:

Are you *managing subordinates?*

Or are you *leading followers?*

If you are managing subordinates rather than leading followers, you may find that the syndromes discussed in the following pages ring true—perhaps uncomfortably true!

A leader is anyone who has followers.
Conversely, regardless of title, you
cannot be a leader without followers!

Memorandum III

Numerous Syndromes Can Get in Your Way

1. The Secrecy-of-My-Job Syndrome

2. The Fill-the-Vacuum Syndrome

3. The Tell-Tell-Tell (or Mushroom Farm) Syndrome

4. The Good-News-Only Syndrome

5. Four Related Syndromes Including the Golden-Rule-of-Power

Item 1

The Secrecy-of-My-Job Syndrome

Have you ever worked in a highly secretive environment? No, not national-security secretive. I'm referring to the don't-let-your-people-know-anything secretive—the kind of environment created by managers who, for any number of reasons, don't seem to want anyone else to know anything of consequence about what is going on. It's little wonder that people in these organizations tell you,

> *The secrecy of my job prevents me from knowing what I am doing.*

Certainly the owner of a small privately-held company may not want to disclose the exact amount of profit earned each year. But the withholding of information can go far beyond the understandable attempts of business owners to maintain some degree of privacy regarding the earnings of their companies.

Many dynamic entrepreneurs reveal only bits and pieces of information to their key subordinates. One in particular was a master at this game. Since he was the only one with the whole picture, he was constantly sought out for even small decisions. How comforting it was for him to be needed so obviously—and to have so many opportunities to demonstrate his decisiveness. And how confusing and frustrating it was for his subordinates to try to perform effectively in the information vacuum!

Entrepreneurs aren't the only ones who have this problem. Many supervisors carefully protect data that may be of substantial interest—and perhaps of some help—to their subordinates. They consciously or unconsciously subscribe to the adage that knowledge is power. By withholding knowledge from their subordinates, they believe that they enhance their own status.

In many organizations, key executives decide against producing organization charts. They generally argue that they want to stay flexible and not be tied down to a fixed structure. This logic, however, doesn't hold up to objective review: If operating relationships change, the manager simply changes the charts.

Many of these same executives avoid job descriptions like the plague. "I don't want my people to have such clearly defined responsibilities that they can say something I want them to do isn't part of their jobs," these executives complain. But they could easily avoid this potential problem by including the statement *Performs other duties as required* as the last item on each job description. A more open-ended final statement is *Performs other duties as requested or as deemed appropriate*.

The challenges faced by an employee who doesn't understand the authority and responsibilities of his or her job are horrendous. How can you, the employee, perform effectively if you don't understand clearly what you are supposed to do? Under these circumstances, how can you fulfill your desires for achievement? Finally, if your responsibilities haven't been defined, on what basis can your supervisor discipline or discharge you?

For the sake of the individual and the organization, everybody deserves to know the answers to certain key questions:

Where is the organization headed?

What is my role in this endeavor?

How is my performance going to be evaluated?

How have I been doing?

Item 2

The Fill-the-Vacuum Syndrome

High school physics teaches that nature abhors a vacuum. So do subordinates!

When people don't know what's going on around them, they become uneasy. They turn to others to share their ignorance and to see if they can learn something—anything—from them. Of course, among their questions of one another is: Why don't they ever tell us anything around here? The question is negative in tone, and the discussions that follow can be expected to go from bad to worse. The situation is easily summarized:

People are down on what they are not up on.

The most fertile fields for the growth of rumors are those in which no sprouting seeds of credible information crowd out the rumors.

Credible information must be balanced information—not just good news. A company that prints only the good news in its weekly keep-them-informed sheet will soon discover its employees tend to discount this approach, finding it offensive or insulting.

When bad news exists, people usually learn of it. At the very least, they sense there's a problem, and in all probability they know much more than secretive managers would like them to.

To the extent that negative information is withheld, all information becomes suspect, which jeopardizes management's credibility. People can handle bad news better when they know and understand its true dimensions. Then, and only then, they can take rational steps to correct its source.

Noncommunicative managers don't necessarily *intend* to withhold information. They may see themselves as good leaders and be relatively unaware of the extent to which their subordinates consider them communicative. These managers should be watching for, and be sensitive to, the signals sent by those with whom they interact.

Item 3

The Tell-Tell-Tell (or Mushroom Farm) Syndrome

The top executives in an organization usually are surprised at the extent to which people at lower levels in the organization believe that communications need to be improved. When the executives find out, they often decide impulsively to tell everyone in the organization what is going on.

What are the first changes to be made under these circumstances? The tell-tell-tell types plunge ahead with a variety of efforts. Some rush into a newsletter program providing a prime front-page location for the president's periodic message. Others have communiques pinned onto the bulletin boards or news inserts added to each person's pay envelope. An investment may be made in slides, movies or video tapes to assure that all employees are exposed to the wonderful story of the organization. One or more of the top executives may even meet with groups of employees to deliver the company's message.

The success of this whole process is keyed to one question: Has anyone at the top of the organization paused to listen to the comments from those in the lower echelons?

Approaches that allow—and preferably encourage—feedback and discussion tend to be received much better than tell-tell-tell programs. In fact, the tell-tell-tell syndrome can be calibrated by the labels various people put on the one-way messages they receive.

The top executives call is *issuing company policies and philosophies and keeping our people informed.*

The second level executives call the process *disseminating the boss's directives.*

The middle managers call it *passing on the party line.*

The first-level supervisors call it *more propaganda from above.*

And what do you suppose the operating-level employees call it? You're right!

Which explains the mushroom farm label. It graphically describes the feelings of people who have to function under a tell-tell-tell administration.

As you can imagine, people who are barraged with information and seldom asked for their own opinions can get to feeling pretty glum about the whole process. So glum, in fact, that the mushroom farm lament may be heard:

> *We feel we're being kept in the dark.*
> *Every once in a while someone comes around*
> *and spreads manure on us.*
> *When our heads pop up,*
> *they're chopped off.*
> *And then we're canned!*

The last two lines are less widely known than the first two—but their reality naturally cultivates the next syndrome.

Item 4

The Good-News-Only Syndrome

A Greek messenger learned only too late about the good-news-only syndrome. His valiant efforts to deliver a message culminated in his being killed. Centuries later the durability of this syndrome was evident from movie mogul Sam Goldwyn's ultimatum to a subordinate:

> *I want your honest opinion*
> *even if it costs you your job!*

One of the most brilliant executives I've ever known couldn't stand the sound of bad news. He seemed to be on a constant high, dynamically striving for new levels of accomplishment. Each benchmark of achievement fueled him to stretch for even higher levels of accomplishment. As the organization grew, the challenges seemed to multiply exponentially and, as might be expected, so did the incident of bad news.

His associates soon learned that they had to pay a high price for leveling with him. Disclosures of bad news brought responses ranging from obvious discomfort or displeasure to almost explosive rage, complete with uncalled for obscenities and ridicule.

Since this executive seemed to want to live in a positive dream world, his subordinates soon learned to always agree with him, never commenting on anything that might cause him to be disagreeable. Those who couldn't accept their apple-polishing role either quit or requested a transfer. Others got fired for insubordination.

Considerable damage was done to the organization during the incredibly long period preceding the removal of this executive. His ability to successfully block the upward flow of negative information to his supervisors led to a pent-up collection of undisclosed problems and served to postpone the executive's eventual removal. When these previously unattended problems erupted, so did career-ending sparks.

When bad news is simply suppressed, the cause does not go away.

Effective supervisors learn that open and constructive disclosures allow them to focus on minor challenges before they become major problems. They also learn that subordinates naturally want to please their leader—and that even a personable leader will receive information which is at least slightly filtered. Consequently, these supervisors strive in every way possible to react constructively to negative information so that their subordinates endure minimal discomfort and feel virtually no fear of dire consequences if they share unpleasant tidings.

Open lines of communications are fostered to the extent that those in positions of authority accept bad news in a calm, professional manner and contribute to appropriate solutions in a constructive way. Those who best understand the total situation are in the best position to succeed.

Item 5

Four Related Syndromes, Including the Golden-Rule-of-Power

A strong directive manager may fall victim to the two-sides-of-every-issue syndrome, claiming:

> *There are two sides to every issue, but I*
> *don't have time to listen to yours!*

The manager who is busy barking orders telegraphs very clearly where listening to subordinates' opinions ranks in his or her priorities—obviously, not very high!

If this attitude elicits words of protest from a subordinate, the manager may emphasize his or her dominant position by exhibiting a symptom of yet another syndrome:

> *If I want your opinion, I'll give it to you!*

Having a boss who is too busy to listen to you is bad enough—but having one who wants to tell you how to think probably is even worse.

Anyone who can be characterized by these two syndromes is likely to succumb to the do-it-because syndrome. This syndrome has a number of variations. Two of the most common are:

> *Do it because I said to.*
> *Do it because I'm the boss.*

This brings us to the golden-rule-of-power syndrome. Whenever I think about it I am reminded of a client who is a very authoritarian manager. Whenever he gets cornered intellectually, he quickly resolves the issue by saying, "Young man, have you forgotten whose name is on that door?" (He is the owner—and it is *his* name, which is also the name of the company, on the door.)

As this story implies, the golden-rule-of-power syndrome is simply:

He who has the gold makes the rules.

These eight syndromes play a significant role in the lives of authoritarian managers. Before we look deeper into the subject of power and its use, review the following list of syndromes and consider to what extent they pertain to your situation.

1. The secrecy-of-my-job syndrome.

2. The fill-the-vacuum syndrome.

3. The tell-tell-tell (mushroom farm) syndrome.

4. The good-news-only syndrome.

5. The two-sides-to-every-issue syndrome.

6. The if-I-want-your-opinion syndrome.

7. The do-it-because syndrome.

8. The golden-rule-of-power syndrome.

Memorandum IV

Power and Its Use
Can Complicate Your Relationships

Item 1

Titles, Status, Authority and Power

While a title doesn't make a leader, it does provide status, power, and authority. But power, like any other tool or resource, can be used, misused, or even abused.

Certainly, anyone with responsibilities wants to have authority commensurate with those responsibilities. Responsibilities without the corresponding authority can be extremely frustrating—particularly if you have the responsibility, and somebody else (such as your supervisor) has the authority.

But what about the negative side of authority? The ability of associates to communicate and develop mutual understanding is essential to an organization's effectiveness and efficiency. But a supervisor's authority to reward and punish subordinates can impair (either consciously or unconsciously) the openness and completeness of conversations.

A very pompous, status-conscious managing director of a European company was referred to as "Mister" to his face and in his absence. His formality and aloofness created almost insurmountable barriers to the development of mutual understanding with his associates. The negative influence of power can complicate efforts to improve understanding between supervisors and subordinates even when the authority figure is sensitive to the issue. And it can pose extreme problems to relationships if not understood—or if abused.

Even for managers and subordinates who work diligently to break down this potential barrier to effective communication, it is virtually impossible to eliminate the barrier. You may have worked for a sensitive, supportive leader whom you learned to respect and trust, and in whose presence you felt quite comfortable. But the fact remains that when the chips were down, the prestige, status, and authority of that manager almost certainly influenced, in at least some little way, your comments and behavior.

Philosophers have recognized for years the potential hazards associated with power:

A leader is best when people barely
know he exists.
Not so good when people obey and
acclaim him.
Worse when they despise him.
If you fail to honor people,
they fail to honor you.

But of a good leader,
who talks little,
when his work is done,
his aim fulfilled,
they will say "we did this ourselves!"

-Lao-Tse

An outstanding leader of more recent vintage observed that:

Leadership is a word and a concept that has been more argued than almost any other I know. I am not one of the desk-pounding type that likes to stick out his jaw and look like he is bossing the show. I would far rather get behind recognizing the frailties and requirements of human nature. I would rather try to persuade a man to go along, because once I have persuaded him, he will stick. If I scare him, he will just stay as long as he is scared, and then be gone.

—Dwight David Eisenhower

The manager who ignores these words of wisdom and flaunts his or her power may achieve short-term ego gratification. But at risk, as Eisenhower points out, are his or her long-term relationships.

Blatant disregard for the complex nature of power and its use or complete insensitivity to the feelings of others manifests itself at best through authoritarian rule—and at worst through open display of anger, which is the next subject.

Item 2

Direct Orders, Fear, and Rage

Perhaps you've heard the story about the executive who was known for flaunting his authority and keeping his associates in a high state of anxiety. He wasn't completely happy with the way things were going for his organization, so he hired a management consultant to help him understand and improve the situation.

The executive called all his key staff members together to tell them of his dissatisfaction and to introduce to them the consultant he had hired to help *shape the place up*. True to his style, he ended the meeting by warning his staff, "Any of you who don't shape up in the next thirty days are going to be fired."

After the meeting the shocked consultant privately coached the executive to move away from ruling by fear and to substitute positive motivation instead. Trying to follow this advice, the executive called another meeting the very next day. It was a short meeting during which he said, "I'm going to try changing my leadership style, so I want you to disregard what I said yesterday. Instead, I want to assure each of you that anyone who shapes up in the next thirty days will be able to keep his job!"

Supervisors wishing to develop highly motivated groups of subordinates who work together as an effective team should be sensitive to the benefits that follow from creating a positive work environment or culture.

People want to be asked to think, not just told what to do!

How about you? Do you enjoy—or would you enjoy—continually being given direct orders with little or no chance to participate in decisions of importance to you? And if *you* don't, why should anybody else be expected to?

A highly directive manager can make a poor atmosphere worse—even intolerable—by venting unbridled anger or rage, as insensitive supervisors so often do. Some misguided managers even believe that in order to acquire or achieve power they need to periodically "chew tail."

But generations of deep thinkers have made different observations.

According to Will Rogers:

People who fly into a rage always make a bad landing.

Rufus Choate observed that:

Power, carried to extremes, is always liable to reaction.

Euripides took a stronger—and perhaps somewhat simplistic or dogmatic position:

Authority is never without hate.

People who are self-confident and widely accepted as powerful leaders generally subscribe to a different approach:

Power is so characteristically calm that calmness in itself has the aspect of power, and forbearance implies strength.
                                                    —Bulwer-Lytton

An authority figure's misuse or abuse of power can result in a number of classic responses, each of which we'll discuss in more detail.

People want to be asked to think, not just told what to do!

Item 3

Three Predictable Responses to the Use of Power

An authoritarian manager who flaunts his or her power may have plenty of subordinates—but may be hard-pressed to find any real followers, without whom he or she can't become a leader.

In all likelihood, such a supervisor will be lacking in followers because of three highly predictable classic responses to the use of power:

1. Fight

2. Flight

3. Submission

Let's examine each of these.

1. *Fight*. When someone is pushed by someone else, the natural reaction is almost always to push back. I have demonstrated this tendency innumerable times in workshops, and have never seen it fail—even when I tried to select an apparently meek person to participate in the demonstration.

How about you? Do you enjoy being pushed around? Has anybody ever given you a direct order that made you feel good?

Over the years only two people have told me that they felt good about receiving a direct order. One, an extroverted vice president of a multi-level-marketing organization, explained that a charming lady once ordered, "Love me!" Another explained that she was once ordered to take a well-deserved vacation that she otherwise would have done without. Both smiled knowingly as they mentioned these exceptions.

2. *Flight*. Most of us don't enjoy fighting—and certainly not a steady diet of it. When faced with a relationship characterized by continual conflict, we try to get away from it. In marriages, people who don't seem able to prevent their conflicts resort to separation or divorce. In organizations, they quit!

People may tolerate an unfulfilling or even unpleasant environment temporarily while hoping that it will change. But as that hope wanes, those who find more promising environments tend to leave. Those who remain, still watching for alternative opportunities elsewhere, may continue to fight back—and risk being fired—or resort to the third alternative.

3. *Submission.* Of the three alternatives, the saddest and most depressing is this one. In some cases, subordinates become almost subhuman. They arrive at work knowing that they will have little or no opportunity to think and achieve except as the pawns of others.

One dynamic but egocentric company chairman kept himself pumped up by picturing himself as almost perfect. To maintain his charade, he needed a scapegoat. An assistant secretary learned to fulfill that role admirably. Admirably? Yes, but how sad.

The assistant secretary played two key roles. Officially, he handled the details in the valleys as the chairman pranced from mountaintop to mountaintop. Unofficially, he played—or at least accepted—the role of scapegoat. His office was adjacent to the chairman's and whenever a problem arose for the chairman—or worse, if an apparent mistake of the chairman's came to light—the chairman would scream, "George!" George (not the assistant secretary's real name) would enter meekly, stand or sit quietly as he was berated thoroughly, and then drag himself forlornly back to his own office. He even was known to quietly accept abuse for problems he had absolutely nothing to do with. Once he even was blamed for something that had occurred while he was on vacation!

A person who submits to such abuse not only lacks feelings of fulfillment, but also becomes an extremely limited resource. In an attempt to avoid conflict and risk, submissive subordinates make little effort to think or to contribute ideas for improvement. Instead, they obediently do what they are told, either building up resentment or blindly trying to block themselves out of any realizations that would foster resentment. Once relegated to the role of nonthinking doers, they can hardly be viewed with high esteem by others—or by themselves.

For the person who is more of a power-wielding manager than a participative leader, the key question is: Which of the responses to your use of power would you like from your subordinates?

Fight?

Flight?

Submission?

When you make your choice from these alternatives, one thing is certain: Whichever you choose—you lose!

Having considered some of the potential problems of a highly authoritarian and directive environment, we can shift our focus to the other end of the spectrum. Participative leadership has the advantage of fostering communication and understanding. But, some managers complain, it may be too soft.

Item 4

Is the Participative Style Soft?

One of the finest executives I've ever known is about as calm as they come. He's also pleasant and somewhat outgoing. During one stage of his career he became president of a floundering division of a major corporation. Before he arrived, the company's sales had stagnated in a declining industry, and pretax profits were only five percent of sales. But in three years under his leadership the company strengthened its management team, increased its sales a gratifying forty percent, and increased its profits by three-hundred percent.

In spite of this outstanding record of accomplishment, at this executive's next performance review the authoritarian group vice president to whom he reported told him that he would not be an effective executive until he got tougher!

What a shame this blood-and-guts attitude is found so frequently in the ranks of management. Whenever a hard-nosed, directive manager raises a question about the possibility that a participative leader may be soft, I'm reminded of how hard people worked under the executive just mentioned.

I'm also reminded of another highly participative leader of a high-tech company in a town known for its university—and for its football team. On Saturdays (including football Saturdays) the company's parking lot would be half full. Even on Sundays, about one-fourth of the lot would be filled. The employees were obviously committed to their work and dedicated to the company.

Unfortunately, the participative leader eventually left the company to form another one, and his successor was a tough, by-the-book, directive manager. Soon after the new manager arrived he made it clear that he intended to *shape up the operation*. But being a fair person, he vowed that he wouldn't ask the engineers and scientists to do anything he wasn't willing to do. And so he punched in and out along with the others on a new time-clock system.

In the new atmosphere people lost their previously high level of morale and commitment. They began working straight eight-hour days, and on weekends there was usually only *one* car in the parking lot. It belonged to the security guard!

Finally, I'm reminded of a newly-appointed manager among a group of scientists—most of whom had been college professors before forming a bioengineering firm. During a leadership workshop this new manager, a scientist who had just been assigned his first subordinates, asked the group, "Do you mean it would be okay for me to talk with my subordinates as if they were my equals?" He was concerned that being too close to his people might be hazardous and that he should stay somewhat removed and aloof so he could make objective decisions. He wanted to appear tough—as a good supervisor should!

What a shame it is for managers to jeopardize their opportunities to be outstanding leaders because they have the mistaken notion that they should be outwardly hard and tough!

The really tough manager is the one who encourages such high levels of commitment and dedication among his associates that they drive themselves to new heights of productivity and quality. The *really* tough manager achieves these levels through astute participative leadership.

Is the participative leadership style soft?

Absolutely not!

Memorandum V

Communication Is the Key Ingredient for Effective Group Effort

Item 1

Lundy's Laws of Communication Within Organizations

Our company's consulting activities include what we call management practices surveys. In such surveys we ask selected managers twenty or thirty questions about their work environment, tailored to the particular interests and apparent needs revealed in preliminary conversations with the executive requesting the study. Invariably, questions about communication are included.

Starting with the person commissioning the survey (usually the president or general manager), we conduct in-depth interviews using the previously selected questions, but posing additional questions as appropriate.

When we start asking about communication, the responses are quite predictable. If the president is asked to comment on communication within the company, he or she is very likely to reply, "Well, they're pretty good. I tell my people everything they need to know."

Whoops! "Everything they need to know" immediately raises a red flag. It is a positive-sounding phrase that often is used by managers who really aren't very communicative.

As the process continues, we interview the people reporting directly to the president. To the question about communication, the answer is likely to be, "Well, in general I guess they're pretty good. I certainly want my people to know everything they need to know—but I sure wish the big boss would keep me better informed."

And so it goes. At each level managers think that they tell their subordinates everything the subordinates need to know, but that they are not well enough informed by their own supervisors.

Lundy's first law of communication within organizations summarizes this highly predictable phenomenon as follows:

> *At whatever level you are in an organization, you feel*
> *that you tell your subordinates everything they need to*

*know—but you wish that your own supervisor would
keep you better informed!*

If we were to interview *your* subordinates what do you think they would say?

In our management practices surveys, we find another interesting and highly predictable phenomenon. We have never worked with—or even heard of—an organization in which people didn't feel there was *significant* room for improvement in the way departments communicate, cooperate, and collaborate with one another.

The salespeople don't understand why the manufacturing people don't respond more cooperatively to emergency requests. The manufacturing people wish the engineers would consult with them instead of designing products that are so hard to produce. The accounting people are unhappy because none of the others turn in their expense reports on time or provide the information requested by the controller.

Consequently, Lundy's second law of communication within organization is this:

*In whichever department you work, you and your
departmental associates wish that the people in other
departments would communicate, cooperate, and
collaborate with you more!*

Lundy's Laws
OF
COMMUNICATION
Within Organizations

Law Number One
At whatever level you are in an organization,
you feel that you tell your subordinates
everything they need to know—but you
wish that your own supervisor would
keep you better informed!

Law Number Two
In whichever department you work,
you and your departmental associates
wish that the people in other departments
would communicate, cooperate, and
collaborate with you more!

Item 2

Communication:
Its Fundamental Importance

For anyone living and working alone, there is no need to communicate. However, the instant two or more people are associated in an organization, the ability to communicate and understand each other is fundamental to their success.

Since supervision must involve at least one subordinate and one supervisor, communication is involved. The manager who would like to become an effective leader will dedicate himself or herself to becoming an effective *communicator* to optimize the organization's performance.

Everything an effective manager does is based on communication:

Planning: Effective managers listen to others' observations about the needs of the organization and its individuals. In discussing alternatives, they seek the insights of others. They evaluate strategies and make decisions based on the concerns of those involved. They delineate, clarify, and communicate goals to others. They discuss and agree on objectives, strategies, and budgets.

Controlling: When it comes time to check progress against previously agreed on objectives, effective managers find out what data to gather. They then share information on what was planned, what was actually achieved, what may have caused any deviation, and what they think should be done about it. They cooperate in taking effective corrective action. They delineate and discuss reporting procedures with both supervisors and subordinates.

Organizing: Effective managers discuss the scope of their authority and the extent of their responsibilities with their supervisors. They learn who to go to for certain kinds of decisions or assistance. When they delegate or accept delegated duties, they clarify who is going to do what. They learn about relationships of individuals and subgroups throughout the organization, and they make themselves aware of plans for either expanding or cutting back the organization's structure.

Staffing: To implement proper staffing, effective managers discuss who can be promoted, where good applicants can be found, and so on.

They recruit subordinates by communicating with prospects about job opportunities. Then they interview candidates and check references. They induct new employees and train others to improve both their performance and their promotability.

Directing: Effective managers participate in daily discussions about assignments, complications, failures, and successes. They explain not only what is expected of subordinates but also how subordinates are doing. The evaluation and discussion of each person's performance is basic to feedback and proper motivation.

Obviously, communication is the logical foundation on which effective leadership is built.

Item 3

The Essential Nature of Feedback, or Looping

Perhaps you have wondered why this book treats the word communication in such an idiosyncratic way. In view of the extent to which people fail to develop high levels of mutual understanding, perhaps we should always put extra emphasis on the first two letters. The point is, effective communication requires feedback, or looping.

It has been said that feedback is the breakfast of champions. Although this saying has broad implications, it certainly is true that champion communicators make sure they understand what the other person is saying.

If I say something to you and just assume that you have understood me, neither of us can be sure complete understanding has occurred. I won't know if you got my message—and neither will you. That is why it is dangerous to assume. Some people like to emphasize the risk of assuming something by trisecting the word assume as follows: Ass-U-Me.

One simple alternative to assuming, of course, is to ask, "Did you understand me?" This question at least opens the door for feedback. It increases the likelihood that a timid listener might venture forth with a response like, "No, I'm not sure I did. Would you explain it once more for me?"

But what if you think you understood me, but neither of us realizes that in reality you did not? For us to be sure you have understood me, more definitive feedback is needed. This can be accomplished if you repeat to me what I have just said—or at least the essence of it. Or, I might look for some action indicating that you have understood my message or instructions.

One basic guideline for effective communication states that

> *It is the sender's responsibility to see that the receiver has gotten the message.*

A good receiver will voluntarily repeat the essence of the sender's message without being asked to do so. But on important matters, a good sender should ask the receiver to provide such feedback or to demonstrate in some definitive way that the message has been understood.

Maybe you don't believe that such efforts are necessary? Many years ago while conducting a communication workshop, I discovered people consistently misunderstood a very simple instruction that I gave. It was quite apparent that I was not communicating the instruction clearly. Rather than improving the instruction, however, I built it into the program as one of the standard exercises in the workshop. I have since given the instruction to several thousand people. When I ask, "Did you understand that instruction?" about 95 percent of the people say "Yes." When I then ask them to write down what they thought I said, about 90 percent of them write something that is absolutely wrong!

Misunderstandings derive not so much from people being more or less smart than others, but because they are *different*. They have different backgrounds, different perspectives, different motives, and different ways of interpreting words. If you understand this and seek feedback in a manner that respects people's differences, you can avoid many misunderstanding.

But what's a little misunderstanding now and then, you might ask. Why bother to seek feedback? Perhaps because, according to a study by the American Management Association, "The average executive spends at least 20 percent of the time coping with misunderstandings."

The most legitimate reason for ignoring feedback is that some discussions do not warrant conclusive evidence that understanding has occurred. However, three less legitimate reasons are sometimes offered:

> *It takes too much time.*

> *The receiver doesn't want to risk being seen as stupid by asking for clarification.*

> *The sender is worried about the possibility of insulting the receiver by asking for a demonstration that he or she understood.*

Can you recall instances when you have not sought feedback because you were concerned about taking too much of an important person's time? Maybe you withdrew from the situation before you had a chance to clearly understand what was being requested. Unfortunately, the person who withdraws prematurely from a conversation with a supervisor often messes up things—and, at best, muddles through.

What about the risk of appearing stupid or insulting the receiver by asking for confirmation? Feedback is a simple matter of good sense, so why should it be considered stupid or insulting? Most people like to know that you are speaking with them instead of at them. And, consider the tradeoffs, such as the potential problems which can arise from misunderstandings and the subsequent confusion and well-founded embarrassment they may cause.

Of course, the way feedback is sought is a key consideration. You might ask any number of questions, including an inoffensive inquiry such as, Charley, I'm not sure I've been able to explain this as clearly as I should; how would you summarize the key elements of this assignment as you understand it?

As Ralph Waldo Emerson observed, "It is a luxury to be understood." However, it is a luxury affordable to all of us—if we are willing to work on it!

*It is the sender's responsibility
to see that the reeiver has gotten
the message.*

Item 4

The Challenge of Listening:
The Adversarial Nature
of Communication

Think about how you feel when you are conversing with others. In a casual conversation you may not be particularly concerned about what you are saying or what you are hearing. We could probably label the atmosphere as neutral.

On the other hand, what is the atmosphere when the conversation relates to resolving some issue or making a decision? How would you compare the effort you devote to making your points to the effort you expend listening to others' points of view?

Do you strain to hear each point being made—and to fully understand its implications?

Or do you concentrate on how best to make your points, how to identify the weaknesses in positions taken by others, and how to counter their points with your own?

Do you search objectively for the truth and an opportunity to increase mutual knowledge and understanding?

Most of us are at least a little careless about trying to understand the points others are trying to convey. And when we interrupt, it's because we are trying to convince others of our point of view.

> *People are usually more firmly convinced that their opinions are precious than that they are true.*
>
> —George Santayana

> *We are by nature stubbornly pledged to defend our own from attack, whether it be our person, our family, our property, or our opinion.*
>
> —James Harvey Robinson

> *Courage is what it takes to stand up and speak; courage is*
> *also what it takes to sit down and listen.*
>
> —Sir Winston Churchill

With the lopsided distribution of power in a supervisor-subordinate relationship, the supervisor has a special responsibility to listen. How patient are you with your subordinates, and how hard do you try to understand what they are trying to tell you?

To what extent do you encourage them to share their views with you—particularly on those matters on which their views are different from yours?

Instead of listening, do you find it easier and more convenient to simply cut them off, snap a quick decision or instruction to them, and get on with other endeavors?

We have identified nine levels of listening. Many of the supervisors we have dealt with in workshops feel that they usually function at levels five, six, and seven—and that they probably could be more effective by shifting into the seven and eight range. At which two or three levels do you typically converse with subordinates? Is there room for improvement?

Level of Listening

1. Not there physically. (You didn't attend or show up.)

2. There physically, but not mentally. (Not paying any attention at all.)

3. Hearing speaker, but doing something else at the same time. (Such as watching elsewhere, reading, or thinking about a different matter.)

4. Interrupting speaker soon and frequently.

5. Interrupting speaker later and less often.

6. Allowing speaker to finish, but meanwhile intensely thinking of a counter argument or response.

7. Allowing speaker to finish while earnestly trying to understand what is being said, and then replying immediately.

8.   Allowing speaker to finish, pausing, thoughtfully consider-
      ing what has been said, and then replying.

9.   Allowing speaker to finish, pausing, summarizing what you
      think you heard, and only then replying.

If you would like to improve your listening skills, the following
suggestions by Dr. Ralph G. Nichols will be helpful (Nichols, R., and
Stevens, L. A., *Are You Listening?*, McGraw-Hill, 1957):

1.   *Listen for ideas and central themes.*
      Search for the speaker's central theme or main points instead
      of getting lost in—or reacting to—the supportive details.

2.   *Judge content, not delivery.*
      Focus, to your best ability, on what the speaker is saying and
      try not to be unduly influenced by his or her way of saying
      it.

3.   *Search for areas of interest.*
      It is extremely easy to tune out a speaker—so work on
      sharing his or her enthusiasm. Selfishly search for new ideas
      or insights which might be beneficial to you.

4.   *Don't jump to conclusions.*
      It's easy to assume that you know the rest of a sentence or
      message after hearing the beginning. Avoid prejudging a
      message, so you can receive and evaluate all of it.

5.   *Take notes, but adjust your note-taking to the speaker.*
      By taking notes you sharpen your reception, understanding,
      and, of course, retention of the information.

6.   *Concentrate—resist distraction.*
      External distractions include nonrelated things you can see
      or hear, or which may be impacting your other senses. Inter-
      nal distractions occur when your mind wanders into unre-
      lated memories or shifts its focus to worries, plans, or
      anticipations.

7. *Use the fast pace of thought to your advantage.*

    Most people can think three or four times faster than they speak. Don't let your quick mind indulge in all sorts of thoughts unrelated to the conversation. Capitalize on your thinking speed by actively sensing, interpreting, evaluating, and summarizing the messages being received.

8. *Check your emotions.*

    It has been said that the intellect is the slave to emotions. Be sensitive to things that trigger your emotions—and increase your efforts to focus on a clear reception and understanding of what is being said.

9. *Exercise your mind.*

    You can turn away from complicated or difficult subjects, or you can intellectually wrestle with complex information so that you will have a chance to grow.

10. *Work at listening.*

    Be an active listener. Follow the above suggestions. Ask questions and seek clarification. Actively share in the sender's efforts to improve your level of understanding, whether or not you think you will agree.

These important tips aside, the most important step in improving your listening skills is to adjust your basic attitude during communication. How wonderful the world might be if everyone shifted to higher levels of listening.

How about you?

As a follower, a leader, a family member, a member of your community, and a citizen—do you have room to become a more effective listener?

Why not give it a try?

Memorandum VI

Associates Can Get Hooked
on Results Through Participation

1. Getting Kicks Through Goals and Achievement

2. Providing Goal-Oriented Involvement

3. Raising Commitment Through Participative Decision Making

4. Goal-Oriented Following: Becoming Part of the Solution

5. The Responsibility to Speak Up

Item 1

Getting Kicks Through Goals and Achievement

Perhaps you've heard that if you don't know where you're going, you won't know when you're lost—or if you have arrived!

Success is often defined as the achievement of goals—in other words, getting where you want to go. Conversely, failure is the inability to achieve goals.

Achievement and recognition for achievement are two of the best motivators around. Therefore, a supervisor should provide subordinates with a chance to seek and achieve fulfillment in their work. But first, the goals of the individuals and the group must be clearly defined, understood, and, to be fully beneficial, accepted as reasonable.

Ambiguous goals and inadequate feedback lead to confusion and frustration. Imagine that you are at a picnic and have an opportunity to try your hand at archery. You select a bow and receive as many arrows as you wish. When you step up to the line, however, you notice that no target is in sight. Then the person in charge puts earmuffs and a blindfold on you so you can neither hear nor see.

What do you do next, and why? Do you stand idle, waiting for further guidance? Maybe you shoot one arrow to at least venture into this crazy game. If you shoot, you would learn what it feels like, but you have no way of knowing if you hit the target.

A situation involving such unclear goals and lacking any feedback would leave you confused and frustrated—and perhaps even upset or despondent. Ambiguity about goals and achievement in the workplace leads to similar results. People need goals so they can correct their actions when targets are missed and so they can feel the deserved satisfaction when targets are hit.

Recognizing these principles, the effective leader:

- Maintains a clear picture of where he or she and the group are headed.
- Inspires others to help themselves and the group get there.

- Understands the value of involving others in the process of delineating goals and evaluating progress.

The best way to meet these criteria is to involve your associates in planning and decision making—and to maintain an open, communicative environment as you set goals, evaluate progress, and repeat the planning and control cycle. When you do so, you practice participative leadership.

If You Don't Know Where You're Going, Any Path is as Good as Another

...but you won't realize if you're lost,
you won't know what time you'll get there,
you might unknowingly be going in circles,
and others won't understand how they can help.
And, since you could pass right by without knowing it,
you won't get the satisfaction of having arrived!

Goals and Achievement — The Bases for Scoring in the Game of Life

Success is the achievement of predetermined goals.

Activity without purpose is like archery without targets or baseball without a home plate to cross.

A sense of accomplishment is the initial reward for achievement of results—and may be enhanced by recognition from others.

Co-achievement is the objective of results-oriented teamwork.

The opportunity to achieve is an incredibly powerful motivator and a key dimension of quality work environments.

Item 2

Providing Goal-Oriented Involvement

Organizations are formed to get results. People are hired to get results. And supervisors and managers are recruited or promoted to get results and to assist others in getting results.

When there is work to be done and there are goals to be achieved, effort is commendable—but *results* are essential!

As Winston Chuchill put it,

> *It is no use saying "We are doing our best." You have got to succeed in doing what is necessary!*

Much has been said and written about goals, management by objectives, and the like. Certainly the underlying concept of goal orientation are fundamentally sound. But often, not enough emphasis is placed on the *process* for establishing and following up on goals.

Goals often are imposed from above. With a little more time and care, those involved in the implementation of goals could be involved during their developmental stages. Then everyone would have a better understanding of and commitment to the goals—and take pride in the achievement of them.

When a goal-oriented system (such as management by objectives) isn't working right, a number of key symptoms appear:

- The people working under the system consider it a periodic exercise rather than a way of life.

- They consider the whole approach somewhat of a nuisance which places too much emphasis on elaborate details and page-after-page of forms.

- They regard the objectives as arbitrarily imposed instead of evolving from participative interactions.

- When the planning cycle is completed (usually several weeks late and into the next year), they wipe their brows and say, "Whew! Now that we've finished that exercise, let's get back to getting the work done."

These problems are not inherent in goal-oriented organizations. They are, instead, problems that good leaders can overcome with communication and understanding.

Under the tutelage of truly effective, goal-oriented, participative leaders, people seek excellence in the pursuit of objectives—and experience high levels of satisfaction when they achieve results. The achievement of predetermined goals becomes not a semimechanical exercise, but an exciting way of life.

According to Thorndike's Law,

Behavior rewarded will be repeated.

The effective leader cultivates goal-oriented followers by rewarding—psychologically as well as materially—goal-oriented performance. He or she helps subordinates evaluate, clarify, and commit to project completion dates, increases in sales, reduction in costs, improvements in quality, higher levels of profits, and all the other results that an organization strives for.

Behavior rewarded will be repeated!

Item 3

Raising Commitment Through Participative Decision Making

The more knowledgeable and competent a manager is in the technical aspects of his or her work, the stronger the tendency is for that manager to make decisions alone—and then just tell subordinates what to do.

Many managers have built reputations as dynamic executives using this authoritarian or directive approach. And many of them have smiled all the way to the bank.

We can only speculate as to whether highly authoritarian people who are successful have achieved their successes because of the authoritarian style or in spite of it.

Numerous other variables—such as intelligence, guts, aggressiveness, energy, persistence, sales ability—may have been even more important than management style. Ruthlessness may even have been a key factor in the success of some. And, of course, some managers happen to be in the right place at the right time—though not necessarily by chance—or happen to have been born into a family enterprise already on the road to commendable results.

One thing, however, is certain. The world has been moving toward increasing levels of self-determination and away from deference to authority simply for authority's sake.

Small countries are seeking more independence from larger countries and empires. Individual countries are increasingly questioning their compliance with the dictates of alliances or cartels. States in this country want freedom to meet their individual needs, and cities often resent the dictates of the states. Even children question more and conform less in the relationships with parents and teachers. And supervisory-subordinate relationships have not been immune to this trend.

Subordinates increasingly ask why. And they increasingly unnerve their supervisors by expecting answers—not just superficial answers, but answers in depth! They want to *understand*.

It doesn't particularly matter whether you believe these trends toward more involvement, participation, recognition, and understanding are good or bad. The fact is that they are real!

What is the significance of all this to the manager? A participative leader who wants to involve subordinates in the decision-making process must consider at least four key points:

1.   The availability of more information on which to base decisions.

2.   The level of commitment by those expected to carry out each decision.

3.   The extent to which good people will be willing to join and remain in the organization.

4.   The opportunity for people at each level to grow professionally.

Let's look at each of these considerations more closely.

1. *The availability of more information on which to base decisions.* Any two people have more information together than either does alone. Galileo said, "I never met a person so ignorant that I couldn't learn from him."

Why is it that Galileo, as knowledgeable as he was, saw the virtue in listening to the ideas of others, yet so many managers apparently don't?

Perhaps some managers feel they are expected to know all the answers—and that they would lose stature in the eyes of their subordinates if they were to seek help and advice. The worst manifestation of this attitude is exhibited by the pretender. But pretending to have the answers doesn't work. Once discovered, the perpetrator loses all the respect he or she was trying to protect.

Nobody expects anyone else to be perfect. And subordinates don't expect their supervisor to be perfect. The manager who honors subordinates by seeking their input will not be seen as inadequate for relying on the knowledge of others, but rather as sufficiently wise and self-confident to make use of subordinates' talents.

Galileo had such wisdom!

2. *The level of commitment by those expected to carry out each decision.* You almost certainly have experienced the imposition of a decision, new policy, new system, or new procedure that you viewed as a nuisance or even a distraction from your efforts to perform well. Be honest. Was the

inherent value of this decision the only issue? In all likelihood, your response was based on an impulse not to conform. After all, who do they think they are, trying to tell you what to do?

A chief executive officer once said that those who will implement the plans should be involved in making the plans. When subordinates provide the necessary input, how can they complain about implementing their own plans?

Say that I am a staff specialist working on a new program for a management information system. I have a choice of seeking user input or not. If I read all the books available on the subject and visit a number of companies to see what they are doing and then lay out my carefully created package for you to follow, you will see it as exactly what it is: *mine*.

On the other hand, if I involve you in developing the new system, it becomes *ours*—not mine. You will see me as a source of help, not as someone badgering you to conform to *my* program.

How can I afford to take the time to solicit your input? Well, the answer isn't found in the old axiom that there's always time to do it over, but never time to do it right. If I don't invest the time to involve you during the creation phase, I will certainly have to spend the time later, during the implementation phase. In fact, those who lack a feeling of ownership or commitment may not only drag their heels in implementing something but may even resort to sabotaging it.

A manager who is perfect may not need to enlist the support of others. However, most of us, occasionally, exhibit imperfections. When you do, do you want your associates to let *your* project fail? Or would you prefer to hear feedback like, "*Our* system had a little glitch in it, but I think I've fixed it so it will continue to work"?

Have you heard the story about the two bricklayers? Both were asked what they were doing. The first bricklayer, who worked under an ineffective supervisor, replied gruffly, "I'm laying bricks." The second, whose supervisor was a communicative leader, looked up with a smile and said, "I'm helping build a cathedral!"

What would you like your subordinates to do? Would you like them to simply help you lay bricks? Or would you like them to enthusiastically help you build cathedrals?

3. *The extent to which good people will be willing to join and remain in the organization.* Earlier we looked at three classic responses to the use of power: fight, flight, or submission. Most people don't enjoy being in a fight, and good people don't have to put up with an atmosphere in which they have to either fight or submit. Instead, they can choose the alternative, flight. In the world of industry and commerce, they go to work somewhere else. The stronger and more capable the person, the more true this is. Good people want to be asked to think, not just told what to do.

It should be no surprise that high turnover often exists in groups headed by people who would rather bark orders than ask questions and listen. The good subordinates, who are the most marketable (and therefore the most independent) will leave. The group is left with the also-rans (inexperienced, incapable, and so on) to fulfill its mission.

In study after study, high turnover often has been traced to inadequacies of supervisors in fulfilling subordinates' *process* needs.

4. *The opportunity for people at each level to grow professionally.* If you are working for me, and I am highly authoritarian and directive, how can you learn and grow? If you can watch me carefully—given the opportunity and the time—you may gather insights in bits and pieces. But until I give you a chance to participate in higher-level decision making, you will not have a real opportunity to gain experience and grow.

It's much the same when finding your way to a new location. If you have ridden with me as a passenger and I have not used you as my navigator, you may well get lost the first time you try to retrace our route. You could learn the route much better if I asked you to help me find the way—or let you drive while I teach you the way.

By enlisting the help of his or her subordinates, a supervisor gives them a chance to learn and grow. And, as a by-product, the supervisor will enjoy improved time management.

I once worked extensively with the president of an insurance company who was trying to improve his time management. Among the issues we addressed was the extent to which he might delegate better. We worked on all the mechanical steps involved in delegating, but the effort was only moderately successful. Then one day, with a warm glow of achievement, he said, "I used to think of delegating as dumping on my people, but I have come to realize that it actually gives them a chance to grow."

How about you? Are you benefiting from the involvement and advice of your subordinates?

Are they getting enough opportunities to think and participate, so they don't have to go somewhere else to find job satisfaction?

And are they getting a chance to grow, so they will become increasingly productive and promotable?

If not, shouldn't you try to make it so?

Item 4

Goal-Oriented Following: Becoming Part of the Solution

Have you ever heard the coaching given by personnel assistants as they help induct new employees into companies characterized by an authoritarian atmosphere? It goes something like this: Around here you don't have to be just a "yes" person. When the boss says no, you say no too! Ouch!

If you and your organization are to prosper, followers need to receive more appropriate advice. Followers need to be encouraged to produce and prosper, both individually and as team members.

If you produce well, will you automatically prosper? Not necessarily, but you will certainly increase the odds in your favor.

Among John F. Kennedy's words, perhaps none received more universal support than "Ask not what your country can do for you. Ask what you can do for your country." Similarly, employers of all types would probably subscribe to these words: Ask not what the company can do for you. Ask what you can do for the company.

Product sales to customers and fees for services to clients provide the revenues from which employment dollars flow. In a free-enterprise society such as ours, the health of a company—indeed, its very survival—depends on its ability to generate revenues that exceed its total costs. This is not just theory or a managerial value judgement. It is a fact of life.

Generating more revenue with a given level of resources or producing a certain level of revenue with a lower level of expenditures is what productivity is all about. It is the path to competitive strength, whether the competition is domestic or foreign.

Many factors influence a company's productivity. Its physical plant and equipment play a role, and so do its people. *All* its people. Managers, first-line supervisors, and operators all contribute to the company's productivity.

It's easy to waste a minute here and there—to arrive a few minutes late for work, extend a coffee break by five or ten minutes, to leave a little early, to spend an excessive amount of time discussing last night's football game, or to keep half a dozen of your associates waiting because you are late for a meeting.

If you were to waste (or cause others to waste) just an hour a day, your company would lose 250 hours per year, or more than 31 days!

It's rather easy to tell yourself that your own productivity doesn't really matter, because your company is big and can afford to carry you in a less-than-fully-productive mode. But what if all the others who work with you feel the same way? If a hundred employees were to adopt your attitude, your company would be carrying one hundred payroll hours per day. In other words, it would be paying for the equivalent of twelve and a half employees who weren't contributing to the health of the company. Hence its ability to provide better pay and more secure careers for those who were contributing would be hampered.

Anyone taking on a new assignment should keep two key goals in mind.

Since he or she is the new kid on the block, the first goal should be to become accepted on the team. It's impossible to overemphasize this point.

In essence, the newcomer should focus on becoming integrated into the organization. He or she should ask questions, seek advice, and offer to help others. The newcomer should not try to appear as a self-appointed expert or hero. Instead, he or she should humbly take the role of a new resource interested in the overall success of the team.

The second goal of a new employee should be to pursue—in every way possible—the successful fulfillment of his or her job, the increased productivity of his or her department or division, and the general success of the organization.

Productivity is based on results—not just activity. Thus it is not enough to work hard. Nor is it necessarily commendable to work long hours. The issue is: What is being accomplished?

You have knowledge, experience, skills—and time. Your productivity is a function of how well you use them to produce results. Look for opportunities to be more efficient. Watch for chances to assist your associates. Talk with your manager about where the company is headed, what he or she considers your role to be, and how you are going to be measured.

As you meld into the team, avoid complaining, drifting, or "serving time." Instead, think positively about the future. Look for signs that your company will succeed, that your associates will share in your mutual accomplishments, and that you will grow professionally.

Some employers are too short-sighted to recognize highly productive people and reward them accordingly. If you work for one, don't presume that his or her deficiency will plague you throughout your career. The many good managers who exist look for results. They therefore are interested in the needs, interests, desires, and aspirations of high performers. And they usually reward good producers—materially and psychologically—beyond high performers' expectations. Serve these managers productively and they almost certainly will reward you accordingly.

Don't let it be said you stopped looking for work as soon as you found your job. Seek an opportunity to be a part of the solution—not part of the problem. Be a contributor. Seek ways to increase your productivity.

Your company will appreciate it.

And your career will flourish.

Productivity is based on results—not just activity!

Item 5

The Responsibility To Speak Up

Not too many years ago there seemed to be an understanding that authority should not be challenged. Students took directions from teachers, and subordinates obeyed supervisors, almost blindly or without regard for the appropriateness of the directions. Vestiges of this attitude toward authority remain, as do expectations that a person of authority should also be well-informed. Some people still feel that a supervisor should be directive and fill a stereotyped role.

But every supervisor should realize that this sort of deference to a power figure substantially inhibits feedback from subordinates. It's probably impossible to create an environment in which subordinates feel completely free to speak up. However, a participative leader encourages openness by being supportive of subordinates and sensitive to the anxieties that impair communication.

One of the more participative leaders among my clients encourages his people with this suggestion:

Don't be afraid to ask dumb questions.

They're easier to handle than dumb mistakes!

Of course, an even more sensitive leader would eliminate the word dumb.

But the point remains that organizational problems often become individual problems, and a supervisor's problems often become the subordinates' too. Subordinates, therefore, owe it to themselves—as well as the organization—to speak up.

Many instances have been observed in which a supervisor and a subordinate either lack mutual understanding or suffer extensive misunderstanding. In such cases at least two people can contribute to improvement. The supervisor can evaluate the extent to which he or she may be creating an atmosphere that inhibits feedback. Similarly, the subordinate can consider the extent to which he or she may be holding back beneficial input. Information and insights that remain unexpressed cannot benefit anyone. And those who hold them in may experience significant frustrations.

Subordinates sometimes misunderstand participative leadership and conduct themselves improperly when a participative leader provides the opportunity to speak up. For their ideas to be effective, subordinates must remain calm and refrain from displaying hostility or impatience.

Some subordinates who give input gracelessly do so to show off or as a means to vent repressed frustrations. Others may have never learned how to interact effectively. Nevertheless, the spirit of participative leadership suffers when the leader's associates are consistently abrasive or antagonistic.

The status-conscious subordinate whose heartbeat and blood pressure rise in the presence of a manager will have trouble communicating, too. Deep breathing before a conversation with an authority figure can relieve these tensions substantially. But in the long run, the subordinate's self-image and self-confidence must be nurtured.

How to Help
Your Manager Lead

- Speak up so others can benefit from your views.

- Present your positions in a forthright manner but be polite and considerate.

- Develop self-confidence strong enough to overcome your anxieties and tendency to defer to power.

Most of all, however, supervisors and subordinates have to realize that communication benefits both. The same is true of all relationships: Undisclosed problems remain unsolved problems. A therapist has told of a patient who had not kissed her husband for many years because he had bad breath. But the patient never discussed the problem with her husband because she feared she might hurt his feelings. Neither one of the couple benefited from the silence.

A magazine editor, whose job is to process letters from people having marital difficulties, made a more general observation. The editor said, "Many people have problems—and one of the things that we've learned is that most of these problems could be solved if the partners would talk with each other." And so it is with the partners known as supervisors and subordinates.

People who want to improve communication, cooperation, and collaboration have an obligation to share their views in an atmosphere of mutual consideration and respect. Otherwise, how can they achieve true understanding?

Memorandum VII

You Can Adopt—and Enjoy
A Participative Leadership Style

Item 1

The New Japanese Management: Neither New nor Japanese!

What has been called the new Japanese-style management is as *old* as common sense, and its success in Japan is generally credited to an *American* consultant, Dr. W. Edwards Deming.

In the early 1950's, Dr. Deming pioneered the implementation of participative leadership in Japan. He envisioned work environments in which management would not only be open to feedback from subordinates but should also actively encourage subordinates to suggest ways of improving productivity and product quality. Suggestions would be evaluated fairly and, when appropriate, would be implemented with substantial support from management.

Dr. Deming's work has been based on the premise that workers have an inherent desire to produce quality products and to do so effectively and efficiently.

In numerous—but still not enough—organizations in the United States, participative leadership prevails at all levels. In these organizations open communication and the opportunity for everyone to think, not just carry out orders, constitutes a way of life.

Other organizations have attempted to implement quality-circle or employee-involvement programs as a quick-fix. However, unless such programs are part of a comprehensive openness throughout the company, they can't be fully effective. The lowest echelons of an organization's hierarchy cannot contribute to progress and achievement if their creative ideas bounce back from middle and upper levels of management like light rays off reflective shields.

Employee involvement at the operating level cannot be fully effective if it is seen by the lower levels of a hierarchy as a system imposed on them by directive managers on high. However, it can be very rewarding if everyone understands and responds to others' desires to achieve and to be recognized.

As Dr. Deming has pointed out,

> *The American worker has nothing but motivation to pro-*
> *duce quality, and can, given the right environment. Em-*
> *ployees and management must agree that they are both*
> *there to provide service that will guarantee jobs for the*
> *future. No country needs to be poor if it has people and*
> *good management. The problem is finding good manage-*
> *ment. People wish to produce quality, they wish to have*
> *pride of authorship.*

Fortunately, many corporations are taking note of Dr. Deming's theories and are providing opportunities for increased achievement and recognition. The challenge is to increase the *entire* organization's commitment to communication, cooperation, and collaboration. Teamwork is the key to achieving higher and higher levels of performance, productivity, progress—and *results*!

Item 2

What If I Don't Have Time?

One of the most commonly encountered excuses for people who have management problems is the lack of time: I don't have enough time to plan; I don't have enough time to go looking for outstanding people or to be cautious in my selection process; I don't have time to induct, train, or delegate to my people, and so on.

Unfortunately, this litany of excuses often includes: I don't have time to ask questions and listen. Particularly listen!

Yet, the people who make these excuses have twenty-four hours a day, seven days a week. The fact is: We all have exactly the same amount of time—not to save, because it can't be stored, but to spend and to use wisely.

If a function or activity has a high enough priority, a person will find time for it. The manager who says—or demonstrates—that he or she doesn't have time to worry about interactions with associates is making it clear that he or she believes other things to be more important. Yet, studies have shown that this same person may spend at least 20 percent of his or her time handling problems that have arisen as a result of misunderstandings.

The earlier discussion of process versus content noted that paying attention to the way something is said or done requires some investment of time. How much time? Usually just minutes a day. The alternative is spending an hour or more—up to 20 percent of the working day—dealing with problems related to misunderstandings.

When a participative leader takes the time to demonstrate concern for his or her associates, the probability of their success—and the organization's success—increases. In the short run, associates will be more supportive of the team's project. In the long run, the participative approach will help weld a team with an outstanding spirit and a high level of commitment to excellence.

How can a harried manager whose life is filled with crises, whose health is jeopardized by anxiety, and who receives less than a full share of appreciation from associates be so blind to the potential benefits of developing and maintaining good (or at least better) interpersonal relationships?

Anyone who is too busy to invest time in sound interpersonal relationships needs enlightenment. And those who fail to achieve such enlightenment deserve our sincere condolences.

Item 3

Four Powerful Words

Several years ago a client whose company had suffered a year without any growth in sales asked if I could do something special for the annual national sales meeting. I suggested that he promise his people that we would provide the finest sales-training program in the world—per word. And what is the finest sales training program in the world—per word?

Ask questions and listen.

We spent half a day during the conference on an approach called consultative selling. The salesperson helps clarify the prospect's needs by asking questions and observes how to best serve the prospect. The salesperson thus serves as a source of help rather than a pitch artist; the prospect gradually moves toward an agreement to buy; and the whole process reduces the risk of subsequent buyer's remorse.

It later occurred to me that there is real power in the four words: ask questions and listen. It also occurred to me that the finest *leadership* training program in the world—per word—probably is:

Ask questions and listen.

So, for the manager wondering how to develop a participative leadership style, my recommendation would be to ask questions and listen! This advice is a natural for any formal interview, whether it be an employment, coaching, or disciplinary session.

The most common mistake made during screening interviews is that the interviewer does too much talking and not enough listening. Similarly, during coaching interviews, supervisors often find themselves doing most of the talking. A more effective approach is to ask those being interviewed to discuss what they know, what they feel uncertain about, how they think progress can be made, and so on. In a disciplinary session, a talkative supervisor risks being seen as not understanding the situation, not appreciating the subordinate's point of view, and making arbitrary judgements. The questioning approach reduces this risk substantially.

One of my most exhilarating professional experiences during the early stages of my career was a one-hour discussion with Joe Wilson, the man who headed Xerox Corporation during its early years of very rapid growth. This particular discussion was intended as a disciplinary session for me. I had been overly exuberant in a particular situation and the result was a minor embarrassment for several of our corporate officers.

During our conversation, Joe asked a lot of questions, and he listened carefully. Through his efforts he guided both of us to higher levels of understanding. We both learned. At the end of the conversation I was sure that he understood my position. I was also thoroughly aware of how I could have handled the situation better. And although the occasion of the conversation had essentially been disciplinary, I left his office feeling better about him than I ever had before. I knew in my own mind that I'd never let him down again. And because of the way he handled the situation, I still felt pretty good about myself.

When you go to a party, you may interact with poor listeners, good listeners, and middle-of-the-road listeners. But at the end of the evening, do you feel good about the highly talkative person? Or do you favorably remember the listener who has asked you about yourself?

In business or in private life, whether dealing with associates, friends, or family members, the most powerful guideline (per word) on how to motivate, inspire, guide, and otherwise interact with others almost certainly has to be:

Ask questions and listen.

Item 4

A Key Word -
Possibly THE Key Word

In the teachings of most religions there is great emphasis on the word love, clearly a word of great importance to each of us as individuals—and to humanity.

The wonders of love and its importance have been described eloquently throughout the ages:

> *Love is the beginning, the middle, and the end of everything.*
>
> —Lacordaine

> *Life is less than nothing without love.*
>
> —Bailey

> *The greatest pleasure of life is love.*
>
> —Sir W. Temple

> *Mutual love, the crown of all our bliss.*
>
> —Milton

Certainly with all its virtues, love can be viewed as the source of great power and hope. According to Virgil, "Love conquers all things."

But can we depend on these assurances? David observed that love must be deserved ("To be loved, be loveable"), and Seneca claimed that it must be earned ("If you wish to be loved, love").

Supervisors may not—and indeed need not—seek love among their associates. But who among us does not seek and relish support, respect, and cooperation from those with whom we interact?

However, in the search for effectiveness, efficiency, achievement, satisfaction, motivation, and happiness, consider the possibility that the most fundamentally important word or concept is not love. In fact, it could well be a word that is a prerequisite to the establishment and maintenance of love itself.

That word is ...

understanding.

In the presence of understanding, all the good qualities of relationships can prevail. In its absence, they don't have a chance.

How about supervisor-subordinate relationships, and the relationships of peers—and the dependence of these relationships on understanding? Have you ever considered the difficulties, hardships, and heartaches that can be traced back to misunderstandings in your own life? Think about how wonderful your world could be if you never had any misunderstanding with your supervisors, peers, subordinates, associates, suppliers, customers, neighbors, friends, relatives, or loved ones.

So what does all this attention to understanding have to do with leadership?

Probably ... *everything!*

On Understanding

Once we achieve mutual understanding, success in our endeavors follows unencumbered.

Nearly all good things (even love) are enhanced by understanding.

Unless I listen better, I'll probably keep on misunderstanding others.

Not interrupting each other will foster improved communication.

Daring to seek confirmation will minimize assumptions and interpretations.

Emotional comments and responses should be dealt with calmly.

Remember the suggestion to use two ears and one mouth proportionately.

Senders should verify that the receivers have gotten the message.

Tell'em what you're going to tell'em, tell'em, and tell'em what you've told 'em.

Active listening can enhance our comprehension of each other's views.

Now that we understand each other better we can proceed to succeed.

Dedication to improved communication requires effort, but can yield great rewards.

Is the prospect of fewer misunderstandings worthy of your commitment?

No effort is more commendable than the search for understanding.

God help all of us to understand each other better!

Item 5

Compliments and Criticism:
The Performer's Scale of Justice

What happens when things are going wrong or when we see someone not following instructions or not performing well? We feel compelled to correct the situation. After all, we don't knowingly want to neglect something that needs to be corrected.

But what if things are going well, or if we catch somebody doing something right?

The natural tendency of most busy supervisors is to presume that whatever is being done correctly will continue to be. So instead of wasting time talking about good performance, supervisors hustle over to do something more important—like correcting someone who is doing something wrong.

When subordinates talk about this imbalance, they make comments like these: "Well, I must be doing okay, because nobody has hollered at me for a week or two," or, "Compliments—what are *they*?"

No wonder the subordinates' lament is

> *We the uninformed,*
> *Working for the inaccessible,*
> *Are doing the impossible*
> *For the ungrateful.*

The sense of imbalance between compliments and criticism is compounded by the fact that most people need more than a pound of compliments to make up for a pound of criticism. So the scale of justice weighing criticisms and compliments is perceived as even more out of balance than it actually may be.

Ridiculous excuses are given for the wide-spread lack of positive feedback. It's not uncommon to hear a manager say something like, Strokes? Sure I give strokes! My employees get thanked every time they get a paycheck. Or, Why should I make a big fuss when something is done well? I *expect* my people to do well. That's why I hire them!

Oh well, not all managers can be good—and none can be perfect! But they can try to become *better*. How about you? Do you see any room for improving the balance between the compliments and criticisms you give?

Positive reinforcement is a powerful phenomenon. It can help your associates glow and grow.

Item 6

Ten Commandments for Maintaining Good Interpersonal Relationships

Many years ago I began reworking a rough draft of an outline which has come to be known as the "Ten Commandments for Maintaining Good Interpersonal Relationships." It was a good outline from the beginning, but it may have become an outstanding one. Its improvement is the result of feedback from hundreds of people.

During the many years in which the outline was used and improved, the suggestions about changing it gradually became less frequent. Eventually, suggestions for improvement ceased. At that point it was "set in stone."

Ten Commandments for Maintaining Good Interpersonal Relationships

1. **Be Friendly and Cheerful.** Be positive in your interactions. Look for the brighter side of everything, and don't unnecessarily burden others with your problems or negative outlook. It has been said that it takes 72 muscles to frown and only 14 to smile.

2. **Speak Less Than You Listen.** Remember that you have two ears and one mouth, and use them in that proportion. Ask questions and listen. Really listen!

3. **Maintain a Calm Manner, Remembering that the Way You Say Something May Be More Significant Than What You Say.** When your nonverbal messages are in conflict with the verbals—the non-verbals will prevail.

4. **Keep an Open Mind and Avoid Defensiveness.** Practice disagreeing without being disagreeable. Seek mutual understanding, not a victory based on argumentation and conflict.

5. **Maintain a Balance Between Constructive Criticism and Praise.** When giving guidance, be sure it is constructive. Watch for opportunities to give sincere praise—and give it. It is often necessary to correct or criticize others—so we do. But just because it isn't necessary to praise others, don't neglect giving praise when it's deserved.

6. **Remember That it is Amazing What You Can Get Done When You Give Credit Where (and When) it is Due.** Avoid bragging, which tends to provide superficial and short-term gratification. You will feel much better if people learn from other—or from your behavior—about your strength and successes.

7. **Keep Others Informed in a Positive Way.** Share insights into potential challenges and opportunities, but avoid promises that you can't keep. When you do make commitments, be dependable.

8. **Avoid Gossip, Negative Comments About Others, and the Spreading of Rumors.** Live so that others' negative complaints about you won't be believed. Don't support or participate in unconstructive bitching sessions behind the backs of others.

9. **Be Sensitive and Considerate About the Limitations, Failing, and Anxieties of Others.** Don't succumb to opportunities for humor at the expense of others. Be compassionate, and give support freely during others' times of need. Be patient and understanding.

10. **Hold Others in High Esteem.** Appreciate others as real human beings with feelings and needs for self-esteem and recognition. Be interested in their thoughts, their circumstances, their families, and their futures.

I could have taken the attitude that the original outline was good, that it was carefully written, and that if some poor soul didn't understand or appreciate it, the outline wasn't the problem.

But I didn't. Instead I accepted the feedback and made changes in the outline. As a result, it was not only improved but it also became a testimonial to the benefits of feedback, the potential contributions of others, and the related virtues of participative leadership.

As is true with *the* Ten Commandments, this set of commandments includes helpful guidelines that you may want to use in the future. It is highly unlikely you will be able to live up to all the commandments all the time. However, periodic review of these commandments will serve you—and your associates—well.

Item 7

Let's Become Outstanding Leaders

This book is dedicated to all who are interested in improving performance and results through better communication and understanding. I hope it will foster a more fulfilling and productive tomorrow for you and that the guidelines on participative leadership will serve you well.

To the manager who would like to become an outstanding leader, or who would like to become an even more outstanding leader, I would recommend reinforcement by occasional rereading of this book.

For more frequent review, read the following outline. It's a handy summary designed to guide any manager to higher levels of leadership.

Let's Become Outstanding Leaders

Listen to your associates.

Explain your thoughts and requests.

Take time to reach true understanding.

Share your goals and aspirations.

Build individual strengths.

Emphasize cooperation and teamwork.

Coach your associates for growth.

Operate with others as if you lacked authority.

Make the involvement of others a habit.

Encourage associates to assist each other.

Observe the good qualities in others.

Underplay your own abilities and accomplishments.

Take others' needs and desires into consideration.

Sympathize with others when appropriate.

Tell the reasons behind your decisions.

Acknowledge the importance of others.

Nourish acceptance of authority and responsibility.

Delegate, delegate, and delegate some more.

Involve others in decision making.

Nominate others for recognition.

Give credit where credit is due.

Let the implementers share in the planning.

Emphatically concern yourself with process.

Allocate your time wisely.

Define expected results and checkpoints clearly.

Expect commitments to be kept.

Review progess fairly.

Search for improvement constantly!

Item 8

Authoritarian Management or Participative Leadership? The Choice is Yours!

This book focuses on the single issue of choosing where you would like to be on the spectrum between authoritarian management and participative leadership—and how to be more participative if you wish.

The authoritarian manager makes decisions on his or her own, directs others to implement them, criticizes quickly and perhaps harshly, and influences by intimidation.

Participative leaders need not be any less concerned than authoritarian managers with purpose, performance, productivity, progress, and results—but their approach is entirely different. They seek the input of others before making decisions. They guide others in implementing. They discuss performance objectively and unemotionally and coach for improvements as needed. They inspire associates to reach for high levels of achievement and encourage their efforts to succeed, and they praise good performance appropriately.

Good participative leaders learn how to ask a lot of questions—not to intimidate, but to learn. They listen, and they are cautious about winning points at the risk of losing relationships. And they constantly strive to seek *understanding*.

Where do you currently consider yourself to be along the spectrum? And where would you like to be?

The Choice is Yours!

About the Author

Dr. Lundy has over thirty years experience in all levels of management, including the presidencies of two multimillion-dollar companies.

He established the recruiting, selecting, and training programs for a small business called The Haloid Company during the years of its most rapid growth. Shortly after he joined Haloid, the name was changed to Xerox. When he left Xerox he had risen to the presidency of its fastest growing division where sales and profits rose 400% in four years under his leadership.

Jim is currently president of Performance Systems, a management consulting company in La Jolla, California. Although his clients have included such giants as IBM, 3M, General Mills, TRW, Hewlett-Packard, General Dynamics, and American Express, his emphasis has been in assisting small organizations to grow and prosper.

Athletic scholarships, a Murphy Scholarship at Northwestern, and a Ford Foundation Fellowship at the University of Minnesota helped Dr. Lundy complete B.S. and M.S. degrees in engineering and a Ph.D in business administration.

Jim's first book, *Effective Industrial Management* (Macmillan, 1957) was adopted by more than a hundred colleges and universities and was also reprinted in India. His second book, *Lead, Follow, or Get Out of the Way*, emphasizes the use of participative leadership in building successful management teams.

Jim Lundy's jam-packed publications and programs focus on key leadership and communication issues for optimizing individual and group performance. His emphasis is on communication, listening, involving others, teamwork, cooperation, interdepartmental collaboration, mutually agreed upon objectives, tracking progress, and improving performance. In other words, achieving results!

Notes

Notes

Order Form

Thank you for purchasing *Lead, Follow, or Get Out of the Way*. To order additional copies of this book or the one described below, please complete the form at the bottom of this page or telephone 1-800-SLAWSON.

Another Avant Leadership Guide:

Talking Your Way to the Top

The Executive's Guide to Public Speaking by John W. Osborne

You will learn how to:

- Rid yourself of fear and anxiety.
- Improve your self-confidence.
- Make your words sparkle.
- Keep your audience interested.
- Be the hit of business and social events.

Name _____

Address _____

City _____ State _____ Zip _____

Qty.	Title	Price ea.	Total
	Talking Your Way to the Top	$8.95	
	Lead, Follow, or Get out of the Way	$8.95	

	Subtotal
U.S. SHIPPING Books are shipped UPS except where a post office box is given as a delivery address.	Sales Tax: CA residents add 7.25%
	Shipping & Handling: $3.00 for first book, 50 cents for each additional book.
	TOTAL

FORM OF PAYMENT

☐ Visa ☐ MasterCard ☐ Check

Card #: | | | | | | | | | | | | | | | | | |

Expiration date: _____

Signature: _____

Mail this order form to:

Avant Books®
Slawson Communications, Inc.
165 Vallecitos de Oro
San Marcos, CA 92069-1436

619/744-2299